STOCKPORT

Yesterday And Today

BY

Memories

Produced for Hammicks Bookshop
Warren St. Stockport

Published by
Memories
222 King Road
Old Trafford
Manchester M16 OJA

Produced for Hammicks Bookshop
2 Warren Street
Stockport SK1 1UD
Telephone 0161 480 7975

Printed by:
MFP
Longford Trading Estate
Thomas Street Stretford
Manchester
M32 OJT

ISBN1 899181 82 2

Produced by NPS
28 Bedford Road
Firswood
Manchester M16 OJA
Telephone 0161 862 9399

Other books by the author:
Stockport Past
Britain in Pictures
Stockport in Pictures
Postcards of Old Stockport.

ACKNOWLEDGEMENTS

To Barry Armstrong for taking the original photographs of Stockport Today.
To Jed McCann for his help, taking the photographs needed to complete today's photography. To Rachael and all the staff at Hammicks for wanting the book, and to Mike Shah of Memories for backing the project. Mike, lives in Stockport, and is always keen to finance and promote publications concerning the history of his home town.

INTRODUCTION

Stockport is one of those towns that has changed very considerably during this century. Tiviot Dale and its railway line and station has gone, swept away by the M60 motorway. Mersey Square and the shopping developments have hidden away the River Mersey, and as we stroll across the square we are unaware of the flowing waters below us. As we pour into Stockport, and park on open spaces and multi-storey car parks, we forget that here is where once huge cotton mills stood, along the banks of the river. And yet, today as always, the market square is where 'it's at', and has been for around 600 years. The church of St. Mary's, Stockport's Parish Church, is still the focal point in the area, and has been for 500 years or more. The vicarage may now be a hotel, the Squire's man-

The author Cliff, with granddaughter Hannah May . . . another Yesterday & Today

sion may be a bank, but some things just stay the same, and they too are recorded here in this book.

Recording the 'today' part of history is not as easy as it sounds. You take a picture today, and by the time your photograph is developed, that view is 'yesterday'. It could be that someone has made single yellow lines, double, a well known shop has closed and become a charity shop, or more parking meters have appeared. Time moves on, with or without us.

As we stand on the threshold of the new millennium, we thought that it would be good to compare views from yesterday with the same view today, showing Stockport as it was, and in doing so, record, for future generations, how the place looks today. And as I have already said, views and photographs of Stockport in 1998 will themselves be Stockport's 'past' all too soon.

So enjoy the comparisons, look for the differences, and marvel at the similarities ....in

Stockport Yesterday and Today.

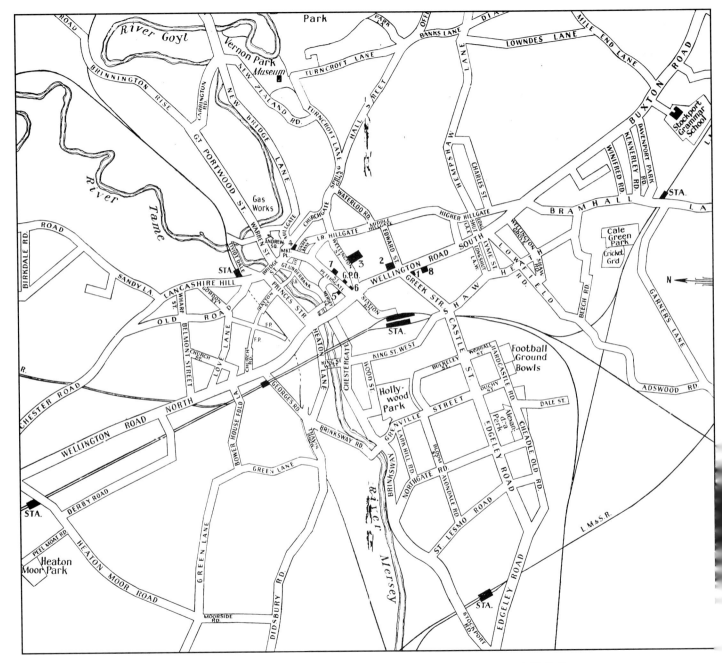

STOCKPORT VISITORS MAP FROM 1932

Stockport has changed more than any other town in the north west during this century. This is because of the culverting and building over of the River Mersey that runs through the town. Older Shopping areas that were busy are now quiet back-waters, and yet the market place has remained the centre. We see above Market place a century ago and below today's shopping centre Merseyway built over the River.

We begin our journey through time in St. Peter's Square and the Parish Church of St. Peter's. Consecrated in 1768 it is a brick built church, able to seat around 460 people. It was recommended for closure in 1969, but saved by the feelings of the congregation. It does have an air of despair about it, especially if viewed from the car park.

St. Petersgate, above from a photograph from c. 1908 with a theatre on the right of the tram. This theatre, that we see here was built on the site of the old Theatre Royal and Opera House and its front dates from 1905. It has had various names over the years 'The Grand', 'Theatre Royal', 'The Empire' and 'Stockport Hippodrome'. Very much a changed view today as we see below. The Theatre Royal was pulled down in 1962 and the offices we see here put up.

St. Petersgate, captured above in the 1930's, when the new large building on the corner of Duke St. was the National Provincial Bank and Prudential Assurance. Still known as Prudential Buildings, built in the late 1920's, it is still there today as our picture below shows.

The Post Office Building, still there. This building opened on October 14th, 1836 and at the time postage was charged by distance, it being 11d (5p) to send a note to someone in London. Our picture above is from c. 1906 and can you see the large telephone mast on the top of the building? Every subscriber had to have their own direct line.

The original caption on our postcard above states that it shows a tram about to climb Daw Bank in 1920. When trams first ran to Stockport it was considered too dangerous for passengers to be on the trams as they climbed this bank, so they had to get off in Mersey Square while the tram made the ascent empty, then picked up passengers in St. Petersgate for the return to Manchester. Below we see the same view today.

This small section of road from Mersey Square up to St. Petersgate has had a variety of names over the years. It's now called St. Peter's Square, though Rock Row and Daw Bank have been used in the past. Above we see a 1960's picture of the No. 74 bus tackling that climb, while below we see the No. 363 to Marple in Nov. 1998. Notice the sign 'Stockport Village' on the building on the left.

Mersey Square, Stockport: above a picture from c. 1930, showing the middle of the Square still open to the River Mersey. Taken from the steps up to Lawrence St., which opened to the public on Aug. 30, 1929, our today picture is taken from those same steps.

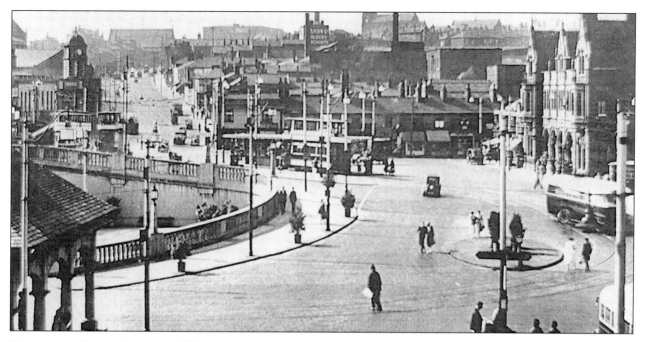

Here we see Mersey Square in 1938 after its first revamp which took place in 1935. The river is now covered and traffic has more room to 'flow'. The fire station is still there on the right. Below we see the only building that was on the Square in our above picture and still there today, the Chestergate Tavern.

Mersey Square, seen from Wellington Road could be in the early 1950's and the Mersey Hotel was still open for a swift half whilst waiting for your bus. Below we see that part of the Square from 1997. Mecca Bingo were still in the large cinema building on the right.

"The Old Bank" says our 1920's postcard, but the original name for the building was Underbank Hall. Parts of the hall go back to c. 1500 and although altered over the years is still a gem in Stockport's history. Built as the town house of the Arderne family from Harden, it was sold to the Manchester and Liverpool District Bank in 1823 by Lord Alvanley and has been a bank ever since. Today, as we see it is in fine shape and owned by the Nat West Bank.

The Market Place, Stockport seen above from a photograph from a century ago. The imposing colonnaded building on the right was started in 1851, and originally just one storey high, and was a produce market. The top storey was added in 1875 and used as a library, and the balcony for public proclamations. The scene today (below) and the Market Hall is still there as is the lovely terracotta building next to it.

Stockport Market Place, a 100 years ago, showing the stalls that stood outside the Angel Inn. You can tell the building that was the 'Angel Public House' by the obvious stone Angels decorating the building. Below we see an unusual picture part of the Market Place on a quiet Sunday morning in 1997. See how uneven the ground is and how steep the climb at the top of Mealhouse Brow.

Market Place and a lovely photo from the early 1930's is shown above. The square is still cobbled and it's obviously a cold damp day. The indoor market hall dates back to 1862 when it was built (without closed sides) at a cost of £4,423 7s. 11d. and was not enclosed until the end of the last century. Still a good place for bargain as we see below from Nov. 1998.

Above we see the Staircase Cafe as it stands today. There is a lot of work to be done on the place if it is to be properly preserved, but we seem to have had those plastic sheets up for years. Good Luck with the project, anyway and mind the ghosts don't get you.

Right we see a lovely view of the Cafe and Woodall's Shop, from a postcard posted Christmas 1904.

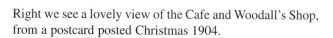

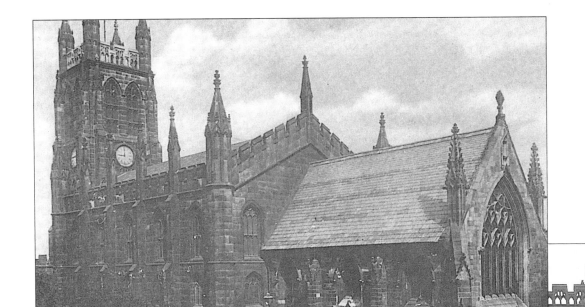

St, Mary's, the Parish and Civic Church for Stockport, that dominates the Market Square. Above we see the church, in a view from 90 years ago. Parts of the church date back to the 1300's, although most of what you see today is from the 1882 restoration, or from when the church was re-built in 1817.

Right: In 1994 I was doing a series of radio programmes, and I invited listeners to join me on a 'Walk Round Stockport'. More than 60 people turned up and we spent a very pleasant Sunday afternoon exploring central Stockport. In this picture we are just about to see the delights of St. Mary's Church.

All churches face the dilemma of dealing with present day life. Roger Scoones, the Rector of St. Mary's seems to have got the bit between his teeth and is facing the challenge head on. The church notice board has been altered and now proclaims that the church 'St. Mary's in the Market Place' is open on "Saturday mornings for tea, coffee and a quiet sit down". Above we see the Rev. Scoones opening up the church, ready to welcome weary shoppers and others interested in the history of the building. Below we see the carved wooden doors of the Legh family chapel in the Vestry.

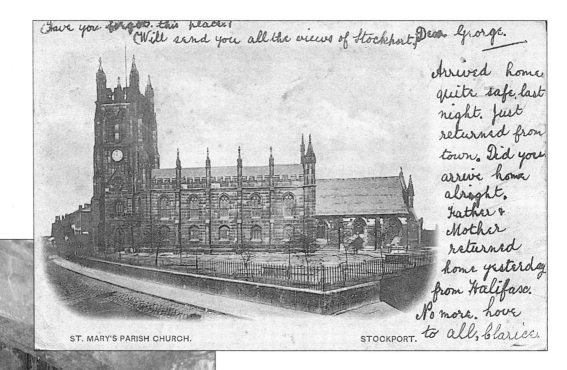

ST. MARY'S PARISH CHURCH.   STOCKPORT.

A 1903 postcard showing St. Mary's Church. At the time all messages had to be squeezed on the front of the card. The gravestones that surround the church had been laid down before the turn of the century.

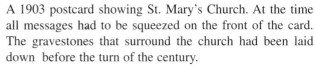

Left: we see inside the Legh family chapel and the red sandstone that dominates the older parts of the church. The family who built and owned Lyme Park would come here on special occasions to say prayers.

Right we see the doorway from the vestry that dates back to Medieval times. The carved heads either side of the door are fine examples of Gothic workmanship. The church suffered a fire in the choir changing rooms recently but is being restored, and will soon be back, even better kept than before.

Left we have some of the fine tracery work on one of the old windows. Churches are primarily for worship, but they are there to fulfil other social needs in society, like recording births, deaths, the lives of prominent people, disasters and wars etc., and if you go in to this lovely old church and take a look at its history, you will be made very welcome, and you will learn quite a lot about Stockport too.

23

Bridge Street, named because it led to Lancashire Bridge, seen above from a 1907 view. Bridge St. Brow and later Briarly's Brow are other names for this steep climb up to the Market Place. This was the original main road into Stockport from Manchester. Where Briarly's is today was once an Inn of ill repute called the 'Hole in the Wall', which was, as the name said just a hole in the wall of Stockport's defences. The pub was known as the King's Arms for a while in the early 1800's.

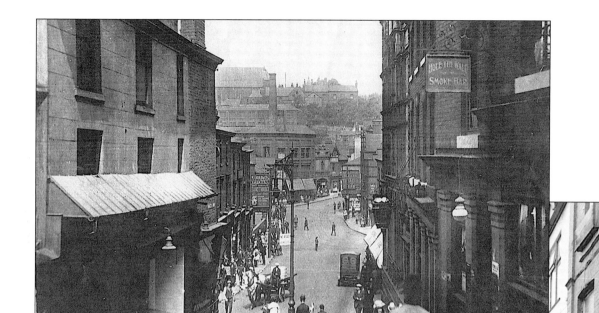

Above we see the Public House called the 'Hole In The Wall' and the scene in Bridge Street as it looked 90 years ago. It must have been a daunting task to climb this last stretch to reach Stockport's market for those carters of the past.

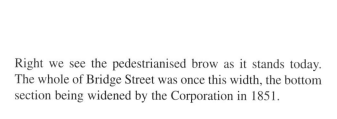

Right we see the pedestrianised brow as it stands today. The whole of Bridge Street was once this width, the bottom section being widened by the Corporation in 1851.

Prince's St, Stockport seen above in a wonderfully nostalgic view from c. 1950 by Valentine Postcards. Actually if you look close they have printed PRINCESS STREET on the front which you, of course know is wrong. This mistake happens a lot, all over the country, and some times the mistake sticks, but not here, thank goodness. Boots Chemist, Dewhurst, New Day Furnishers, Redmans; all the names from the fifties are here in this busy shopping street. How much it has altered in our view of the same spot today, below.

Prince's Street, in 1949. As the trams were gradually cut back and phased out the 'end of the line' for some services was in Prince's Street and above we see the tram staff 'having a quick drag' before turning the tram round ready for the trip out to Reddish. Below we see the same spot today and how the nature of the shops has changed over those 50 intervening years.

Prince's Street got its name when George, Prince of Wales, visited the town on July 1st, 1908 to open Stockport's Town Hall. He, with the Princess of Wales and a large and Royal party, arrived at Tiviot Dale Station and proceeded in carriages to Wellington Road. As the Royals passed down what was then Heaton Lane, council workmen pulled a string and signs proclaiming Prince's Street fell over the old signs, renaming the street. It is still a shopping street as we see below, but not supplying the necessities of life as it once did.

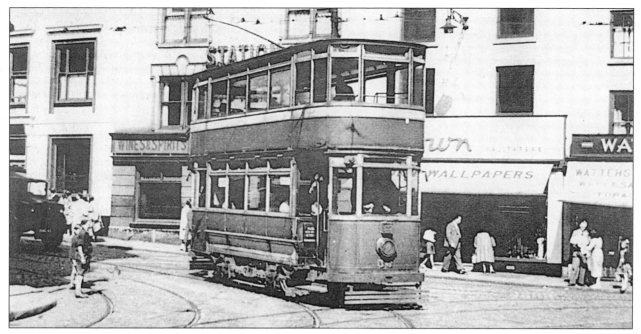

At the end of Prince's Street, where it joined Lancashire Hill, was Tiviot Dale Railway Station. Because this was an important entrance to the town it was well served with trams and cabs. This made the Tiviot Dale/ Prince's Street corner a busy one and above we see a photo from c. 1950 of that spot. Today it is a quiet backwater, useful for parking, well out of the main flow of traffic. Crown Wallpapers has become a bookies, the Station Hotel has gone, but as we see below from 1997, the Station Hotel is still there, complete with its ghosts.

Bridge Street, Stockport in 1920, is what we see above. The number 62 tram passes the Buck and Dog Inn as it makes its way out to Hyde. The scene today is shown on our picture 'today' that is below.

Lancashire Bridge was for hundreds of years the main way into Stockport and a very important crossing of the River Mersey. Above we see Bridge Street and Lancashire Bridge as it looked in 1922 and below the same stretch of road, though looking the opposite way, as it is today. It looks as if the traffic could almost retrace the way it came in the past, but today's buses etc, have to turn, left or right, at the bottom of Lancashire Hill.

Stockport's Fire Station, boarded up and ready for demolition in 1964. The building had opened on April 10th, 1902 and replaced a fire station on Corporation Street. That same view today is shown below, and this is one of those photos that is hard to believe. Everything has gone, it looks completely different, but that's how it is.

The Fire Station, Mersey Square in c. 1911. This view shows the tram sheds to the right behind the Fire Station, where the Merseyway shopping precinct is today. It is always perplexing when an area is swept away and completely replaced, as happened in Stockport, but the same view today is shown below.

Wellington Road North as it looked in the 1920's on our photograph above. The road today, though looking the opposite way is the view below.

The White Lion Inn, Stockport, as it looked in 1905 is shown above while today's view is right. From 1730 until the coming of the railways in 1839 this was THE Inn place in Stockport. The London Mail coaches arrived here, the post arrived here and the gardens of the Inn stretched down to the River Mersey, where you could go salmon fishing. Patrons at the Friday night disco may wish to be reminded that it was here we have our last recorded 'wife selling' in Stockport. Friday March 25th, 1831 William Clayton sold his wife to J. Booth for five shillings (25p).

Left St. Petersgate bridge was built in 1867 and open to the public on February 24th that year. Prior to that the only way from St. Petersgate to the market or St. Mary's church was down a steep slope into Little Underbank and up some steps into the Market Square. A lot of visitors to Stockport do not realise that there are steps down from the bridge into Little Underbank, tucked away, they were constructed at the same time as the bridge. A few times up and down there each day would keep you fit.

Right we see the view off the St Petersgate Bridge looking towards Great Underbank

Since the St. Petersgate bridge was opened in 1867, it has been one of the most popular and recognisable views in the town. It is this view was see above from 1904 and all its Edwardian bustle, and below, on a quiet Sunday morning 1997.

Left we see the view of the Little Underbank, but this time taken from on the bridge at Easter 1997.

Right we look at the bridge from the other side, from the start of Lower Hillgate. The postcard is from 1950 and shows cars parked outside the shops.

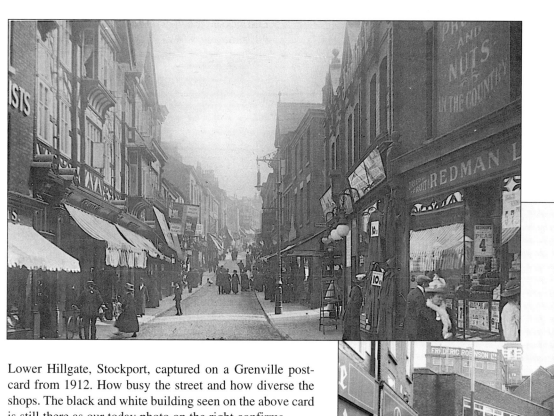

Lower Hillgate, Stockport, captured on a Grenville post-card from 1912. How busy the street and how diverse the shops. The black and white building seen on the above card is still there as our today photo on the right confirms.

Mersey Square just after it was first re-built, in 1935, while below we see that basically, this part of the Square has not really changed since then. The old buildings beyond the bridge have gone and so have the trams, but the lamps and balustrade is still in place.

The Armoury, Shaw Heath seen above at the turn of the 1900's with the Amoury Inn next to it and Watters, tobacco blenders across the road. The Armoury and the pub are both still there, on the corner of Greek Street, as our picture below from 1998 shows.

There are 80 years between our two pictures of the Florist Hotel, Shaw Heath, yet so many of the buildings are the same in both pictures. Above we see the Longshut Lane junction in 1915, and below from Nov. 1998.

The Church of Our Lady and the Apostles at Shaw Heath shown here on a 1929 postcard. Below we see the church undergoing a facelift and repairs from Summer 1997 in the corner of the photograph, though the view is dominated by the Swan Inn and the Armoury public house.

Castle Street, Edgeley, showing the road leading away from Shaw Heath as it was in Edwardian times. The street today is cut off and pedestrianised at this point today as we see below.

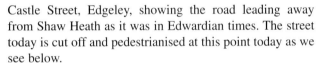

Two pictures from the past, and both from around 1960. Above we see a single deck Leyland bus waiting to leave for Marple Bridge on a service run by the North Western Road Car Co. Below we see a Stockport Corporation bus on the 27 route just coming into Mersey Square.

Stockport Corporation bus no. 24 on service 24 to Adswood, via Garner's Lane in 1965 and the conductor (remember them) is having a quiet smoke before tackling the passengers once more. Stockport Corporation Transport Department would not allow advertisements on the sides of their buses as they said it lowered the tone of the town. I wonder what they would have thought of today's transport system with buses of every colour flying round the town and even windows painted over, just to get bigger adverts on the buses.

Tiviot Dale Railway Station, seen around 1960. The station had opened on Dec. 1st, 1865 by the Stockport, Timperley and Altrincham Junction Railway Co. and the name was spelt Teviot with an 'e'. Until 1948 the station was part of the Cheshire Lines Comittee then part of British Rail. The building behind the station above was the Hanover Independent Chapel, nicknamed by Stockport 'The Methodist Cathedral of the North'. Below we see B1 class engine 61394 emerging from the tunnel that ran under Lancashire Hill, on the Manchester Central to Sheffield Midland train in May of 1965.

(photo A. W. Steele, courtesy of Locofotos).

The line that ran through Tiviot Dale station was very well used and popular for excursions to the seaside, and holiday specials. The line was also a major freight route, and even when passenger services were withdrawn on January 2nd, 1967 under the axe of Dr. Beeching, freight trains continued. In 1980 an accident involving a crane, building the new Stockport-by-pass, closed the line. It should have re-opened, but it never did, and the road, now the M60 swallowed up the railway. Above we see L.M.S. engine 44851 on one of those freight trains coming into Tiviot Dale on the middle through line. below the site of the station today, looking east of the Lancashire Hill bridge.

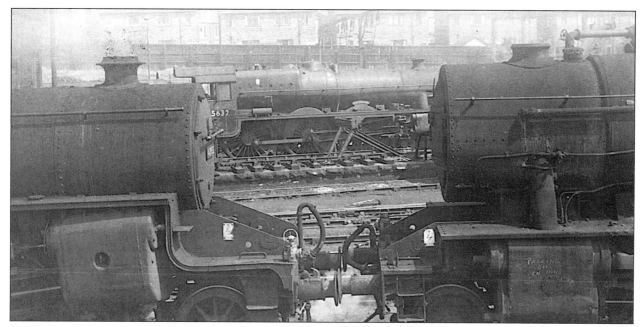

The Stockport area has more than it's fair share of railway lines running through it, and many locals worked on or were connected with the Railways. There was once a large marshalling yard just off George's Road (where B & Q stands today) and sheds at Edgeley, Heaton Mersey and Portwood. Above we see a well composed photo featuring Jubilee class engine 45632 'Tonga' framed between L.M.S. 'Crab' 42932 and Standard 90712 on Edgeley shed in June 1964. Below we see 42772 and 42941, waiting, May 1965, in Edgeley sidings, to be taken away for scrap, after being withdrawn.

(photo A. W. Steele, courtesy of Locofotos).

92033, a powerful British Rail freight locomotive hauls a Crewe freight train through Edgeley junction on June 5th, 1958. While today 80% of all workings in the area are multiple units, either diesel or electric. Below we see an E.M.U., just coming off the viaduct, on its way to Crewe in November 1998.

(photo A. W. Steele, courtesy of Locofotos).

Above we see one of the L.M.S. 'Royal Scot' class 46160 "Queen Victoria's Rifleman" on duty taking the 'Comet' express down to London in the late 1950's. Whilst below we have electric loco 86260 'Driver Wallace Oakes G.C.' bringing in an express heading for the north.

A fine view across the Stockport viaduct as 86260 prepares to leave Stockport station, November 1989. The engine will soon be removed as the train is to head over non-electrified lines north of Manchester. The viaduct was built in the years 1839-40 and was officially opened on December 21st 1840, with two rail lines. It soon proved not capable of handling all the rail traffic that was developing between Manchester and the south and another viaduct was built alongside the original one in 1889. The viaduct was cleaned and renovated in 1988.

Left we see what Stockportians see all the time, a plane overhead. Wherever you are in the centre of Stockport - look up and you will see a plane, as the town lies on the main approach to Ringway, oh I'm sorry, Manchester's International Two Runway Airport.

There seems to have been building work going on some-
where in Stockport for most of this century that is now
drawing to a close. Above we see the scene at the bottom
of Exchange Street, looking across at the end of Daw Bank
in the summer of 1965. The line had recently been electri-
fied, though freight and local workings were still steam
hauled as we see in our picture, with Black Five no. 44677
on parcels duty. Right we see the bus station that is there
today.

53

Stockport has revived a wonderful piece of heritage by bringing back to life the air-raid shelters cut in 1939, into the soft sand-stone that the town stands on. They are well worth a visit and there are a thousand good stories attached to these 'havens of safety' beneath the towns of Stockport. Right we see one of the town newer landmarks, the glass pyramid, that lies alongside the M60. They say that working under a pyramid shape sharpens the mind (and razor blades), who would you suggest to move in there, instead of the bank who own it at the moment?

A close-up of the famous figures that once fronted Winter's jewellers in Little Underbank. Today the figures now over a century old and the famous clock are well preserved and the building is a restaurant. Below we see one of the forgotten buildings of Stockport, - the Court House on Warren Street. Not forgotten is Hammicks bookshop next door and it's friendly staff.

The festive Season and Christmas will never be the same, since they closed the Davenport Theatre down. For many years I would take the family, every New Year's Eve to the Pantomime there. We had a lot of pleasure from the place and watched, John Inman, Les Dawson, Roy Barraclough, Russ Abbott, Ken Dodd and many more kept the audiences in fits of laughter. Opened in June 1937 as a cinema/theatre, it is seen above just after it opened by Mayor George Padmore. Below we see the Davenport just before it closed on March 10th 1997 because Stockport Grammar School, who own the land, wanted to build on the site and Appollo Leisure said the building needed too much money spending on it.

Today another of Stockport's great 'Palace's of Entertainment' stands empty. I wonder how long it will be before the Plaza falls victim to the hand of fate. Built in the late 1930's, and with seats for 1,873 customers it was once one of Stockport's most luxurious cinemas. The cinema closed in 1966 and it took a year before it opened as a Mecca Bingo Hall in 1967. That too has closed and the signs taken down, so what will happen to the Plaza?

Right we see the statue, erected by the people of Stockport to Richard Cobden, who for a time was their M.P. It was unveiled by his daughter Jane, on Nov 27 1886.

57

Talking of heroes, the lads that put Stockport F.C. in the Second Division and playing the likes of Manchester City, must come close to local heroes. Here we see the reception on a cold day in 1997 when the team toured the town after winning that promotion.

THIS TABLET WAS ERECTED
BY PUBLIC SUBSCRIPTION
IN MEMORY
OF
HOWARD BECKWITH,
SUPERINTENDENT OF THE
STOCKPORT FIRE BRIGADE
FROM 11TH JUNE 1892
WHO WAS KILLED NEAR THIS PLACE
WHILST PROCEEDING TO A FIRE ON
THE 29TH DAY OF DECEMBER 1926,
AT THE AGE OF 64 YEARS.

DURING HIS CAREER HE WAS AWARDED
THE SILVER MEDAL AND THREE BARS OF THE
LIVERPOOL SHIPWRECK AND HUMANE SOCIETY,
THE BRONZE MEDAL OF THE ROYAL HUMANE SOCIETY,
THE BRONZE MEDAL OF THE R.S.P.C.A.
THE KING'S POLICE AND FIRE BRIGADE MEDAL,
THE LONG SERVICE MEDAL WITH TWO BARS OF THE
ASSOCIATION OF FIRE BRIGADE OFFICERS,
THE MEDALLIONS OF THE ST JOHN AMBULANCE
ASSOCIATION; AND THE ROYAL LIFE SAVING SOCIETY.

THESE AWARDS MORE THAN ANY WORDS, TESTIFY
TO THE MANY SERVICES WHICH HE GAVE WILLINGLY
BOTH IN HIS PUBLIC AND PRIVATE CAPACITY.

"WELL DONE, THOU GOOD AND FAITHFUL SERVANT."

As well as a statue, Stockport has a couple of plaques, the one right commemorates Howard Beckwith, and his unfortunate death in 1926. Stockport could do with a Millennium plan to put up a few more statues and definitely some more blue plaques to the heroes of the town's past.

(photographed dy CRISPIN EURICH)

Those of us who term ourselves local historians always walk in the shadows of those who have gone before. Stockport has had some very good historians in its past and I hope there are some to come. Me, I hope I've helped matters along, filled a small space and placed a brick in the wall of knowledge of the area. My favourite photograph of Stockport is actually of Lawrence Steven Lowry, stood on the steps down to Daw Bank bus station, looking at the viaduct and the River Mersey flowing away below. That's L.S. above and me to the right. Same spot, 50 years between the photos.

Above: The spot where the River Mersey starts. Hidden today beneath the M60 it is where the Rivers Tame and Goyt join. Below: The Mersey leaves Stockport and flows away in time.